I0211021

She Loves me,
She Loves me Not

poems by

Madari Pendas

Finishing Line Press
Georgetown, Kentucky

She Loves me,
She Loves me Not

Copyright © 2025 by Madari Pendas
ISBN 979-8-88838-973-7 First Edition
All rights reserved under International and Pan-American Copyright Conventions.
No part of this book may be reproduced in any manner whatsoever without written
permission from the publisher, except in the case of brief quotations embodied in
critical articles and reviews.

ACKNOWLEDGMENTS

With gratitude to Rodrigo Miragaya, whose steady encouragement and
luminous spirit have meant more than words can say.

Publisher: Leah Huete de Maines
Editor: Christen Kincaid
Front Cover Art: Madari Pendas
Back Cover Art: Rodrigo Miragaya
Author Photo: John Parra
Cover Design: Elizabeth Maines McCleavy

Order online: www.finishinglinepress.com
also available on amazon.com

Author inquiries and mail orders:
Finishing Line Press
PO Box 1626
Georgetown, Kentucky 40324
USA

Contents

"*I knew it all along. There is no one who can stand the freedom of others; no one likes to live with a free person. If you are free, that's the price you have to pay: loneliness.*"
—*Chavela Vargas*

"*When you love someone in secret, do you fail to love them?*"
—*Julia Koets*

Tortillera

Cubans call queer women, *tortilleras*,
tortilla makers/lovers/experts.

I can't remember the first time I heard the word,
but I remember the scorn, the spittle,

a word where the teeth dig into the lips
like white enamel gravestones.

Why is it bad to love tortillas?
Why are women always given second names?

The Virgin Mary has appeared
as a burnt accent on tortillas,

hands clasped, the downbeat of an applause,
eyes turned away in modesty.

Maybe she lays her image on tortillas
to send a message.

A holy visit, like Jesus visiting disciples.
A tortilla, flat, pock-marked

like a moon, foldable, a miracle gripped
between burnt brown hands.

I'm shoved by my granny at the market
for hugging her for too long, lingering on her neck,

People will think we're tortilleras, get off.
I pray an apology.

I didn't know any act of affection
could be read as gay.

Looking back, however, I wonder
if that's what she thought because

she wrestled with those desires
as well, reading them everywhere,

even in her grandbaby,
in her hugs.

Once, me and my dad were trying
to sneak her gift under the Xmas tree & to

distract her while my dad moved
I kissed her

on the lips,
and held myself there as my dad

tiptoed to the tree.
Her eyes were wide, shocked;

the lip skin dry, flat,
like scritta paper.

What did she think
during that pause?

What ideas about me
were permanently formed that day?

I'm disgusted now by the act.
Why did I think to do that?

I was six, maybe younger,
but at the time it didn't seem wrong—

It's sacrilegious to touch your saints,
even their garments are off-limits.

My grandma, head hung low, embarrassed,
crossed-arm, she moved to the papayas,

a fruit & a word my people use for vaginas.
I never ate any when she brought the sliced segments,

cut and moist, watery on the plate,
ripe when soft,

an orange-amber skin,
black seeds whispering out.

But I did eat some in secret,
hunched over the sink,

my prayer hands closed &
tight like a votive flame.

The papaya's juices puddled underneath, the seeds like
the beads of a rosary clustered, waterfalling,

making a *tin-tin* sound against the
metal mouth of the sink,

rolling & collecting
in the drain.

I ate of the fruit like that first woman, fallen,
yet I closed my eyes to enjoy the syrupy pulp—

deviations are made in darkness—
scraps of moon shone through the window slats,

pale, gray light illuminated the soft cavity,
my tongue traced its clefs and hills,

its peaks and valleys, kissing
with gentle precision that low cavern, what is holiest,

making a covenant with my body,
letting the saliva run down my lips and chin,

sated.

Sleepover

As lovely as the first night of summer,
we're allowed to lay together.
I know I won't sleep tonight.

It's all girls & we fill the room
with strawberry, peach, violet.
As lovely as the first night of summer.

Couldn't this be our world?
Just us, our laughter, our games.
I know I won't sleep tonight.

All our moms said yes.
Her sleeping bag is next to mine.
As lovely as the first night of summer.

My breath fogs her glasses &
I can smell the mint on her teeth,
I know I won't sleep tonight.

We gab until cicadas sing,
her small arm rolls onto my back.
As lovely as the first night of summer.
I know I won't sleep tonight.

My First Queer Teacher

Twin dimples on each cheek, like end points
on a bridge. A traversable smile. Deep set
hooded eyes, almond slits that roved
and roamed, regarding the desks. I try to guess
her age and feel cruel at this attempt.

She seems both ageless and experienced,
knowledgeable & preserved in innocence,
pickled in an exquisite, timeless brine.
Gay in a past I supposed wounded her,
transported her across coasts, life spilling

from her tan valise. In search of life,
an extraterrestrial, hoping for hospitable soil
& potable water, a place in which to reveal
her dimples, her secret, folded flesh,
a clef in the sand, made & unmade by waves.

Love is her philosophy. For books, for writing,
even for the unwilling, talkative-note-passing
students. From one side of the room to another,
projector to board to desk to our huddle groups,
moving like time: at once passing, and at once

frozen in an eclipsed gaze, like all firsts.
I want to be her; I decide as she lectures.
She lets her grays show, delicate straight
caramel hair flanked by rooks of silver.
I can be this, I can be happy.

I can be happy. I can be this.

Gay

Gay
Adjective.
1. "Bright, lively."
2. "Keenly alive and exuberant: having or inducing high spirits."
3. "Given to social pleasures." Also: LICENTIOUS.
4. "Of, relating to, or characterized by sexual or romantic attraction to people of one's same sex."

Noun
5. "Sometimes disparaging + offensive; see usage paragraph below: a gay person especially a gay man."

—Merriam-Webster Dictionary

(1)
The cafeteria
is bright & lively
with the vim & vigor
of children.
We sing & shout,
imitating the macaws
we saw hovering over
the live oak,
pomegranate-red plumage,
brilliant, honorable,
we all tried to call it
to our forearms,
as if we could
command or control
nature.

I hear the word
first as an insult,
in the cafeteria,
breaking through the din,
three tables down,
lunch almost over.
I look for the mouth,

but everyone's chewing
& talking & Kate C.
is asking me about a sleepover.

You're so gay!

I hear it again,
I swivel out of my seat,
to find the voice.
I don't see the speaker
but the receiver:
Mike R.
His head is set
over his crossed arms.
His flat pizza & tater tots
uneaten, cooling.
I know this face,
I know any face
on the verge of wailing.

(2)
Mike & I
used to chase
iguanas until
they skittered
up the sabal palm,
disappearing
into the green scrub.

We felt exuberantly
& brilliantly alive,
dashing towards
a group of lounging
lizards, their red
dewlaps, flashing,
warning us to stay away,
until they bolted

into the cavern
of a gutter.

Were we drawn to one
another,
able to sense
the jitteriness
of the other's secret?

(3)
When summers
reached 105 degrees,
Mike & I retreated inside,
afraid that we'd literally
melt—we had watched
the *Wizard of Oz* together,
each aping the Witch's death,
flat on our bellies,
puddled ladies.

We wrote notes
to people in our class
on construction paper,
trying to make smooth-edged
hearts with pink safety scissors.
They were invitations
to a fancy tea party;
we'd even get real,
non-caffeinated jasmine tea.
I'd wear a top hat.
Mike said he'd borrow his mom's
slick, thick pearls.
It'd be splendid,
splendid;
puddled ladies.

(4)
I don't know why I
thought this, but
as we entered high school
it felt like being gay
was somehow worse
for boys.

Boys seemed
riotous, louder,
a thick tangle
of muscles & hair
& fists.

We, girls, were
allowed
to sleep close to one another,
to even practice slipping
our tongues into one
another's mouths.
And still be straight.
Mike disappeared first year,
transferred,
transformed,
maybe it was too much.
He had been caught
in the student parking lot
behind a Tercel,
knees graveled.
licentious.

(5)
In the elementary cafeteria
the other boys
finish off his food,
flinging some torn
tato bits at his head,

a scrap smacks his lip,
then rolls down his philtrum,
then chin.

He looks down,
already defeated—
for some reason,
I think if he had called
the macaw over
it would have come to him.

Petunia

Her petals in the bathtub swirl
the water around us, her fingers make laps

& ripples, each body a shore, a determinable
end for the waves we pulse back-and-forth.

Here we can hold hands without fear.
Petunias without sun will not bloom,

true of her as her namesake, her back
& shoulders a pollock of new freckles.

I run the rag along her neck,
tracing its meridians,

she tells me
that petunias as a gift mean anger,

not all flowers make good presents.
She re-ties her hair, recently Kerotin-ed,

but the ends have already begun to curl & twist,
the strands that aren't swept up

I wash, watching the ironed flatness,
the artificial straightness slowly crimp.

We dry, re-petaled in the towel's
spindles of cotton, to bed.

We have no names for what's to come:
the hand that reaches over in bed

between my breasts like a safety belt,
her breath against my nape, as if

she too was trying to see my curl pattern,
bringing forth the natural & hidden waves.

Ms. P Tells us to Stop

Darla and I
hold hands,
Ms. P stops the class/
eyes fixed/pointed/glowering/
at us.

Ms. P petite/Texas/Blonde/
hypnotically & aggressively
white/ surprised/
This is our judge.

She examines
the two delicate
hands wrapped
in one another's
like the healing
snakes on Caduceus.

It's a drama class,
so we've come
to expect spectacles/
melodrama/ faux faint spells.

Darla and I vine & graft
on to each other.

Why are y'all holding hands?

Ms. P asks, arms akimbo,
class won't resume
until we answer/
confess/cry/or change seats.

I wish I had a good/proper
answer for her,
but how can I admit
to a whole class

how much I want
to kiss Darla,
raise both our hands
towards her long/
elegant/smooth neck.

How?

Our laced fingers
hang over the edge,
as if trying to dive/
escape/ hide.
Ms. P is silent
until we pull them
apart. The digits
sliding out of the gaps
they've closed.

Ms. P
waits for our
apology/
waits for the shame/
lesson/guilt
to show on
our faces.
Sorry, one of us says—
after this will Darla
ever want to hold
my hand again?
Does this kill
her desire/love/questions?

Class resumes,
Ms. P talks about
Hamlet,
she reminds us she played
Ophelia/ drowned girl.

Under our laps
I search for
Darla's fragile
hand, hoping
whatever we have
is not over.

She gives
only a crooked pinky
and we hook
them together,
tangled
fishing lines,
twisting/
pulling/
knotting/
under Ms. P's sights,
by our thighs—
a flesh rebellion,
a small, swinging
insurrection, &
that's when I learn
the most important
lesson:

love doesn't stop,
it simply
learns how best
to hide.

Questions After Seeing a Beautiful Woman on 32nd Ave

Has she taught herself to laugh
at small pains?
Does she kiss her scrapes?
Does she blanche or rouge
when eating spicy foods?
Does her tongue hang out like a shirt tag?
Does she cover her mouth
with her palm when she laughs?
Does she check her horoscope
before leaving in the morning?
Did she ever stick a penny
in the gaps of her dimples?
Did she ever eat a worm
in school on a dare?
Did she think all cats were girls?
And all dogs were boys?
Does she love the spirals in her hair?
Or iron them out vigorously
each morning, breathing
in the steam of the rising heat?
Does she pray or curse
when she's afraid?
Does she kiss bread
after it falls on the floor?
Did she talk into the fan
to sound like a robot?
Did she see me?
Would she have loved
the way I lick my plates
after a meal?
Or giggle when I tell
her I used to eat ketchup
packets?
Am I someone she could
love?

Or someone that could
make her stop
on the street
on a rainy Wednesday
and ask a million
questions?

Believing and Knowing

Tabitha,
slid her glasses
down before kissing me.
I felt my pulse in my lips,
or maybe it was her pulse;
she had given it to me, along
with a question I spent
my life smothering.
I searched for her in all my loves.
Sometimes I got close,
I felt a tickling,
not a fire, or searing,
but an ember,
trickling down my spine,
orange and bright,
tumbling through my fleshy parts,
knocking
against the knuckles
of my vertebrae.
With her I disappeared,
with men I
became even more present,
more aware,
of every movement,
discomfort,
unwanted touch,
as if all my skin had eyes,
like aspen trees,
and was repudiating me.

Finally

My date moves
the curls out of my eyes
& speaks so low
I lean in to hear her.
My only thought as she jumps
over the center console,
straddling me is:

Finally—fucking, finally—

I didn't realize how long
I had been waiting,
twenty-three years,
dying of thirst &
so unaware
of being parched.

Finally—

This life is possible,
it's not a dream. Her hands
move up to my chest,
& I revise all my beliefs,
I believe in nothing,
no bearded Gods or Sheols,
nothing save for this woman's next
touch, next giggle, next
moan, next bite,
next command
in the shadowed
car lot
beneath the banyan tree.

Finally—

My lips necklace her:
neck, long, smooth,
then her chest,
violet lipstick smudges
eddying from her clavicle
down her chest,
ribs,
pelvis

Finally—

I'm stunned by what I'm bold
enough to do in the dark;
her eyes—lustful slits—
look me over.

The lambent streetlight
falls over her,
why did it take this long?
Will it always take this long?
If I lose her,
will it be another twenty-
something years again,
before I'm allowed
to feel this alive?

I lean in again,
fevered by her gaze,
by her invitation,
by the squeak of the seat
as it reclines,

Finally—fucking, finally—

Pansies

Let	you	live
always	on	the back

of
a
pretty
girl's
ear.

Performative Bisexuality

Booze changes her stare,
her eyes are glass rims

        filling with wheat & hops,
        spume of desire dribbling over the glass, rushing.

What changes occur in her that finally
allow her arms to scarf me?
        For her lips to loosen
        and pox me?

When we drink we're effusive,
cradled & swaddled by hot throat Henny.
        We learn to love the smoldering
        in our mouths & uvulas,

allowed to become,
we set ourselves on fire
        just to watch and wait for the other
        to smother the flames.

We can love like this, the boozy
skin torching us, the brown rivulets
        running down our chins,
        followed by a tongue's parallel.

        Then, unfortunately, morning. Mourning.

& she retracts like a bad instinct
when I kiss her the next day, our hair
        tangled together in a matted nest,
        faces on the pillow waiting to

mix like bourbon and sugar,
as if the gap between our faces,
        that silk trail, that border,
        needs to be closed, redrawn,

made so it ends where my
philtrum begins,
        the clef she buried & unearthed.
        she gave easily what today she reviles.

I try to kiss her, but her hand blocks. STOP.
I am mistaken, she turns to sleep
        in space without my face, without
        my breath, without my immigration.

She says she remembers nothing of the night,
combing the kinks in her hair with her fingers,
        those acrylic tines that raked my neck
        when she poured herself into me.

Hair of the dog? Beer on the nightstand. Am I this desperate
for love? For the love of someone
        who finds me a novelty? Barefoot
        she leaves; a voice turned scuttle.

We are not "together." It's simply fun. That's all.
As the liquor leaves, so does her form.
        Under the strobing lights, fluttering
        dance-floor confetti, surrounded by cheers

and gawking that is when she can love me,
when others, men, in their own chaffed minds
        can approve. She can only kiss me
        when there's applause.

Medusa Goes Down on Me

but her snakes keep biting me. "They're not poisonous," Medusa says, reminding me and apologizing with a hand that strokes my knee. My thighs have twin punctures all over, pinhole eyes. When we first tried to hook up, I said they looked like wall outlets. "Plug in, baby," I joked, trying to be cute, trying to make the stinging in my legs less obvious. It's hard to be in a relationship where you can't look your partner in the eye, but I think Medusa prefers it like that. There's something more intimate about a stare. Sometimes I try to guess her eye color. Green? Blue? Hazel? Maybe she's forgotten. She's not one for mirrors. If she looks at herself, she won't turn into stone—that's a bad rumor. No, she doesn't like seeing how she's changed or seeing how the snakes stare at themselves as well, so much alive beyond her. I'm not sure if she thinks of them as children or siblings. It's probably more like a parent-baby relationship. She's canceled some of our dates to go to PetSmart to buy live mice, little white-science-experiment-buggers. When I went with her once, the snakes glared at a corn snake, pressing their pyramid heads against the glass, tapping out some code. Were they jealous? Or curious as to where this snake's human was? I try to focus on the pleasure, Medusa's tongue moves like a snake's, quick, light—there's something airy about each flick, as if she's savoring and not committing. The thing is—I don't believe I deserve to feel good. I try. I close my eyes, tight. So tight I see eddies of green and blue and sometimes violet—maybe her eyes are violet, like Liz Taylor's. One of the snakes breathes on me, then lies flatly on my pelvis, tired. This is when I learn that each one has a personality of its own. There are ones in the back that knot and fight and Medusa must be thoughtful about how she parts her hair, keeping them separate. There are the three that bite and hiss and sometimes wrap around my throat when Medusa and I kiss—maybe they think if I die, they can have my body. There's one that looks like it's constantly whispering in Medusa's ear. "Does this feel good?" Medusa asks, shaking her head, and it does, fuck, dear God it does—I feel a tingling in the soles of my feet. "Yes, it does, babe." But then I remember my guilt, the fact that we're both women ripe with shame, women who look down when men enter rooms, cursed women. Maybe

I don't think I'm allowed to feel good after breaking my family's heart. "Monstrous," my mother shouted. "Disgusting." My father looked at us (eyes not meeting Medusa's of course) as if trying to work out the logistics of how we actually fuck. Or maybe trying to work up the courage to ask her if she has pubic snakes. (She doesn't). She doesn't let anyone touch her. When I try to make a path, lips bouncing down her flesh alley, I feel her whole body say "no." Medusa keeps looking for new ways to be punished, as if her suffering needs compound interest. It seems selfish to be happy in this world. What would happen if she orgasmed? Would the snakes feel a second-hand pleasure, throbbing then falling limp? Maybe they'd stop biting me if they knew I could make them feel good. Maybe they would stroke my arms, or massage my quads, perhaps they'd simply watch, waiting. Make us feel good. Make us feel God. "Are you close?" she asks, her voice muffled. Turn me to stone. I want to be something beautiful and eternal, I think. My parents could visit me without worry. We could finally have a relationship. One of old temple worshipping. It'd be easier to be a stone woman. Ageless. Perfect. Quiet. At least then I wouldn't care about the strings of blood on my legs or whether my stomach looks fat when I'm naked or about being choked or dying in some airless nuclear strike. I would no longer disappoint anyone. "Look at me," I say, asking for the most supreme of pleasures. And from between my legs, feral and damp, she does, she looks at me— brown—they are—dark brown—

Queer and in Public

Perhaps it was our wild curls,
like brown flouncing halos,
or the deep coral of our lips,
darkened by secret kisses,
the overwhelming pull
towards one another, two crescents,
wholed; holed up in a corner booth,
sill in disbelief that *this* could
really be our lives.

Perhaps someone caught the flay
& flip of our hands.
D kept with the affection,
nibbling at my neck, whispering,
sitting side-by-side, a hand on
the ripped hole in my jeans, traipsing,
twirling the frayed threads,
slipping under the fabric, a promise.
She wanted to never hide,
to never love in secret again,
but I pulled away.

Perhaps it was the look on my face.
People will think we're...you know.
It was my voice, but really
an imitation of my mother's.
A restrained shame.
I wiped my neck & cracked
the chop sticks,
snapping,
separate.

Perhaps it was bound to happen.
We noticed every worker,
chef, busboy, dishwasher,
had come out to watch us,

standing by the hostess' table
under the red paper lanterns,
whispering what we might have been:
sisters, of course, a waitress insists.
I saw them kiss. Ain't no sisters.
Friends? Good friends?

Perhaps it was curiosity and not hate.
I didn't think we could exist either.
Wouldn't I, under a false guise,
also have stared and gawked
and refilled the water
until it spilled on the tablecloth,
the red fabric darkening
as if it were bleeding,
a radiating hemorrhage?

Red Tulips

I hear the yes as if it weren't really spoken. It's as if we have ventured into a dimension of non-language, telepathy, Jung's Collective Unconscious. My incredulity must have been so obvious that she repeats herself, *yes, yeah*. Her hand is as small as mine. I hear the door opening. It's real. This is really her home, her bed, her nightstand with an earmarked crime novel, her hands removing my sundress. I waited so long for this moment. I want to hear what else she has to say: the sounds of her body, of pleasure, of pillows, of drawers opening to grab toys, of sheets, of glee, of laughter. The sounds women make are pleasure themselves. I hear her next command and I can't get there fast enough, and then I tumble, as if I'm falling through myself and out of myself, every neuron and synapse firing, and I just listen. I hear *yes* again, over, and over. *Yes, yes, yes, yes. Yes.*

Madari Pendas is a Cuban-American writer and interdisciplinary artist whose work explores the surreal dimensions of exile, the layered complexities of Latinidad, and the intersections of language, memory, and identity. She holds an MFA in Fiction from Florida International University, where she was a Lawrence Sanders Fellow.

Her debut book, *Crossing the Hyphen* (Tolsun Books, 2021), examines Caribbean heritage and familial mythology through the lenses of immigration and bilingualism. Pendas's genre-defying writing has earned recognition from the Academy of American Poets, Florida International University (in fiction, poetry, and creative nonfiction), Arkana, and others. She is a two-time Pushcart Prize nominee.

Her prose and hybrid works have appeared in *The Masters Review, CRAFT, Miami New Times, SmokeLong Quarterly, The Louisville Review, The Florida Book Review, South Dakota Review, Salamander, The Rumpus,* and elsewhere.

Pendas has lived and taught in France—across Île-de-France, Fontaine-le-Port, and Toulon—bringing an international perspective to her work. As a visual artist, her paintings and illustrations have been featured in *Sinister Wisdom, The Flagler Review, The Courtship of the Winds,* and numerous literary platforms. She has also designed book covers and creates both impressionistic works and narrative-driven cartoons and comics.

She currently resides in Miami with her partner, Rodrigo, and their beagle, Cluey.

www.ingramcontent.com/pod-product-compliance
Lightning Source LLC
Chambersburg PA
CBHW022057080426
42734CB00009B/1381